Wittgenstein

FOR BEGINNERS

John Heaton and Judy Groves

ICON ◆ BOOKS

First published in 1994 by Icon Books Ltd.,
52 High Street, Trumpington, Cambridge CB2 2LS

Distributed in the UK, Canada, Europe and Asia by the Penguin Group:
Penguin Books Ltd., 27 Wrights Lane, London W8 5TZ

Published in Australia in 1994 by Allen & Unwin Pty. Ltd.,
PO Box 8500, 9 Atchison Street, St. Leonards, NSW 2065

Originating editor: Richard Appignanesi

ISBN 1 874166 17 X

Printed and bound in Great Britain by
The Bath Press, Bath

He was born Ludwig Josef Johann Wittgenstein on 26 April 1889, the eighth and youngest child of one of the wealthiest families in Hapsburg Vienna. His father Karl (1847-1913) was of Jewish descent (Karl's father had converted to Protestantism). His mother Lepoldine Kalmus (1850-1926), known as "Poldy", was a Catholic. Ludwig was baptized in the Catholic Church.

The father's immense wealth as a leading figure in the iron and steel industry, known as "The Carnegie of Austria", enabled the family to live in the style of the aristocracy. Their home in Vienna, in the Alleegasse (now Argentinergasse), was known as the Palais Wittgenstein. In addition, they had a house on the outskirts of Vienna and a large estate in the country.

The Wittgensteins were at the centre of the cultural life of *fin de siècle* Vienna.

Brahms

Mahler

Kokoschka

Klimt

Schiele

Ludwig was brought up in a house of music. There were seven grand pianos in his childhood home. The composers Brahms and Mahler were frequent visitors to the musical evenings, and young Pablo Casals played there. A brother became a very well-known concert pianist. When Karl retired from industry, he became a great patron of the visual arts. Aided by a daughter, a gifted painter, he collected works of Klimt, Schiele, Kokoschka and Rodin.

I₇

Ludwig, like his brothers and sisters, was educated privately by tutors and governesses. He was quiet and obedient but had considerable practical talent.

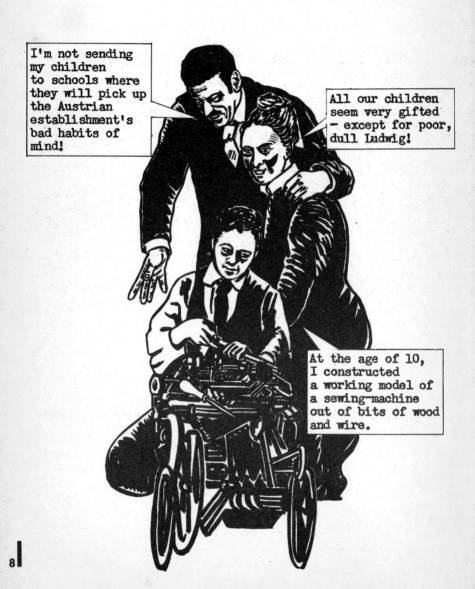

I'm not sending my children to schools where they will pick up the Austrian establishment's bad habits of mind!

All our children seem very gifted — except for poor, dull Ludwig!

At the age of 10, I constructed a working model of a sewing-machine out of bits of wood and wire.

At the age of fourteen, he was sent
to a rather unacademic school at Linz.
Adolf Hitler, who was almost exactly
the same age as Ludwig, was also there.

When he was seventeen and a half, Ludwig went to study mechanical engineering in Berlin at the *Technische Hochschule,* the most renowned of German engineering schools, where he completed his diploma course. During this time he started writing down thoughts about his own life, a practice he continued for most of his life.

If my notebook is to be in order, I must, as it were, step straight out of doors from it — into life — and not have to climb up into the light as if from a cellar or to jump down onto the earth again from a higher level.

ENGINEERING IN MANCHESTER, ENGLAND

In 1908 Wittgenstein went to Manchester as a research student in Engineering. He stayed there for three years.

He was interested in aeronautics. He began his research by experimenting with kites. Little was known then about conditions in the atmosphere.

He went on to do experiments on the combustion of high pressure gases and then he became interested in the design of propellers. This requires mathematical treatment and so he got involved in the study of the foundations of mathematics.

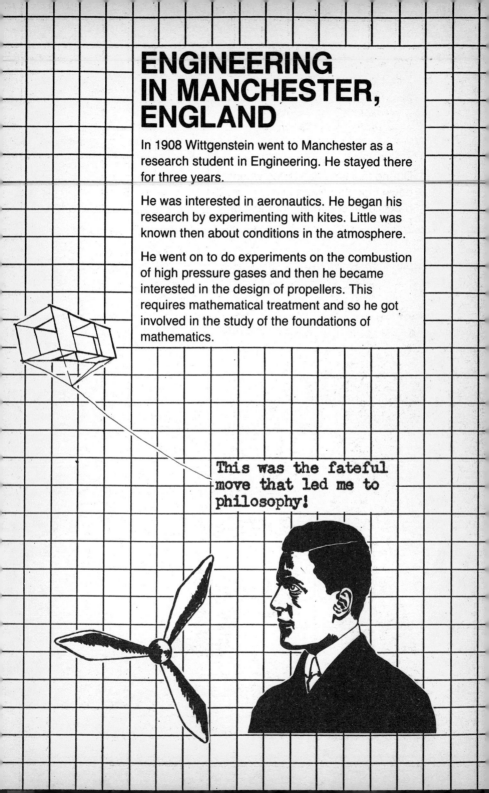

This was the fateful move that led me to philosophy!

CAMBRIDGE UNIVERSITY

So Wittgenstein went to Trinity College, Cambridge, to study under Bertrand Russell (1872-1970) who was a lecturer in mathematical logic. This was to lead to a passionate intellectual friendship between these two great philosophers in which both were transformed. Russell came from a distinguished aristocratic family. He was now forty and had finished *Principia Mathematica,* one of the most difficult and important philosophical books of the 20th century and was world famous amongst philosophers. Wittgenstein was twenty-two and completely unknown, although very wealthy.

BERTIE WITH MOUSTACHE

Russell suggested he write an essay during the vacation on any philosophical subject. He did so, and when Russell had read the first sentence, he was persuaded that Wittgenstein was a man of genius. Russell later wrote . . .

He was perhaps the most perfect example I have ever known of genius as traditionally conceived, passionate, profound, intense and domineering.

He would visit Russell at midnight, pace up and down like a wild beast for hours in agitated silence, wrestling with problems of logic and with his sins.

I feared to suggest it was time for bed — because if I did, I felt he might blow out his brains!

Russell came to love Wittgenstein "as if he were my son" and had to reassure his mistress, Lady Ottoline Morrell . . .

Wittgenstein moved swiftly from being a protégé to being Russell's master, for he made phenomenal progress. Russell was writing a huge work on the Theory of Knowledge which he showed Wittgenstein.

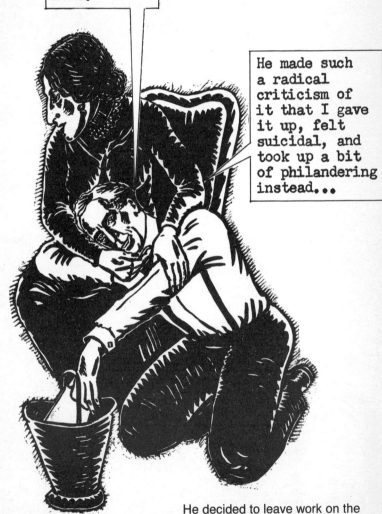

Of course, Otto darling, I love you more!

He made such a radical criticism of it that I gave it up, felt suicidal, and took up a bit of philandering instead...

He decided to leave work on the fundamentals of logic to Wittgenstein.

Although Wittgenstein was obviously a difficult man to get on with, he made some good friends at Cambridge. One of his closest was David Pinsent, a man of his age who could calm him down, play music and go on holidays with him.

He was killed in an aeroplane accident in the war. My TRACTATUS is dedicated to him.

An important friend was J.M. Keynes (1883-1946), the economist, who quickly recognized Wittgenstein's ability.

I remained his friend all of my life...

SOLITUDE

In 1913, Wittgenstein decided to live for two years in Norway on his own to meditate and work on logic. Russell tried to dissuade him.

It will be dark.

I hate daylight.

You'll be lonely.

I prostitute my mind talking to intelligent people.

You're mad!

God preserve me from sanity!

God certainly will!

So he went to live by the side of Sogne fjord, north of Bergen.

But Wittgenstein had not got his B.A. degree. So Moore, who was now a friend, visited him in Norway and took down a series of notes on logic that Wittgenstein dictated.

You know, these notes will do for a BA thesis.

Moore, on returning to Cambridge, found out that the regulations required that the thesis contain a preface and references, and he wrote to tell Wittgenstein this.

Your letter annoyed me. When I wrote Logic I didn't consult the regulations, and therefore I think it would only be fair if you gave me my degree without consulting them so much either!.... If I am not worth making an exception for even in some STUPID details then I may as well go to HELL directly; and if I am worth it and you don't do it then - by GOD you might go there.

Moore understandably was furious and did not reply, so Wittgenstein did not get his degree.

THE FIRST WORLD WAR

Soon after the 1914-18 war broke out, Wittgenstein joined the Austrian army as a volunteer gunner and was sent to the Eastern Front.

Since his adolescence, Wittgenstein had often thought of death. He had a morbid conviction that he would die soon and had no right to live unless he created some great work.

On his first glimpse of the enemy he wrote...

Now I have a chance to be a decent human being for I am standing eye to eye with death.

For the first two years of the war, he did not see much action, although he suffered from the harshness of the conditions and the brutality and futility of the war.

I knew from the start that our side would lose!

In between his duties, he continued his thoughts on logic which he put down in his notebook, together with thoughts about his spiritual state. He read Leo Tolstoy's *The Gospel in Brief* and was deeply influenced by it.

His father had died in 1913, leaving him a large fortune. He had given much of this away to Austrian poets and artists in need of money. These included Georg Trakl, Rainer Maria Rilke and Theodor Haecker, the translator of Kierkegaard. In the winter of 1914, Wittgenstein received a note from Trakl (1887-1914), one of the greatest of Austrian poets, to visit him in Krakow where he was in a military hospital as a psychiatric patient.

At nightfall the autumn woods cry out
With deadly weapons and the golden plains,
The deep blue lakes, above which more darkly
Rolls the sun; the night embraces
Dying warriors, the wild lament
Of their broken mouths.
But quietly there in the pastureland
Red clouds in which an angry god resides,
The shed blood gathers, lunar coolness.
All the roads lead to blackest carrion.
(from ''Grodek'' by Trakl)

Winter is setting in...
Once again no clarity
of vision. Yet I am
obviously on the
point of solving
the most profound
problems, so much
so that the solution
is practically
under my nose!!!
The thing is,
my mind is simply
blind to it just
at this moment.
I feel that I
am at the
very gate but
cannot see it
clearly enough
to be able to
open it. This
is an extremely
remarkable
state which
I have never
experienced
so clearly
as at present.

(Diary 16/11/14)

In March 1916, Wittgenstein was posted to a fighting unit on the Russian front as an ordinary soldier. In June, Russia launched its major assault, and so began some of the heaviest fighting in the war. Wittgenstein's regiment faced the brunt of the attack and suffered enormous casualties. He, by his own request, was posted to the place where he was in most danger, the observation post ahead of the front line where he could survey the enemy guns.

If I lose heart or flinch when I hear shots—that's a sign of a false view of life...

Perhaps the nearness of death will bring me the light of life. May God enlighten me. I am a worm, but through God I become a man. God be with me. Amen.

He was awarded the first of several medals for bravery. His notes indicate that a radical change had occurred in his thinking. He began to grasp how his thoughts on logic connected with his concern to live rightly.

and the form '$\xi.\eta$' as

Yes, my work has broadened out from the foundations of logic to the essence of the world.

He was made an officer
and was involved in
more heavy fighting.
At the end of the war, he
and 300,000 Austrian
troops were made
prisoners by the Italians,
and 30,000 were to die
in captivity of disease
and starvation. Both his
family and Keynes
worked to obtain his
release, but he refused
to go until the last of his
men were released.

Typhoid has
broken out at
the Other Ranks'
camp at Cassino—
I request a
transfer THERE!

But he had finished
the **Tractatus,**
the culmination of his
thoughts on logic
and ethics.

Wittgenstein sent the **Tractatus** to several publishers who rejected it, including his own university press — Cambridge, which was to distinguish itself by rejecting all his writing. His later work was published by an Oxford publisher. In 1922, he at last got it published with Russell's help, but was paid nothing for the rights of the book and entitled to no royalties from its sales. It soon became a classic.

TRACTATUS LOGICO-PHILOSOPHICUS

The Tractatus, a classic of 20th century philosophy, is a short book, about 70 pages, consisting of remarks on the essence of language, the nature of the world, of logic, mathematics, science and philosophy, and ending with comments on ethics, religion and mysticism.

It is written with logical precision and often poetic intensity.

Its tone seeks to convey an unmeasurable dimension which makes possible a proper ordering of both experience and action.

The book is not a textbook giving information about Wittgenstein's philosophical opinions. As he wrote in the Preface: "Its purpose would be achieved if it gave pleasure to one person who read and understood it."

It is to be read as an initiation, drawing a limit to the expression of thoughts by expressing what can be said as clearly as possible. "The more the nail has been hit on the head — the greater will be its value."

TRACTATUS LOGICO- PHILOSOPHICUS

BUT WHAT REALLY MATTERS IS WHAT WE CAN ONLY BE SILENT ABOUT

The book is structured as an organic whole. Wittgenstein was critical of systematic thought in philosophy which built itself up from foundations. Strictly speaking, there is no beginning or end to the **Tractatus**. We start in the middle! He shows this by making the first and last sentence interdependent.

The first sentence goes:

THE WORLD IS ALL THAT IS THE CASE

And the last:

WHAT WE CANNOT SPEAK ABOUT WE MUST PASS OVER IN SILENCE

The last sentence assumes that only factual propositions are meaningful, so the world consists only of facts. But the first, in stating that the world is all that is the case, presupposes that the world *is,* which is ineffable in the sense of the last sentence.

A single thought, namely the distinction between what can be **said** and what can only be **shown**, is being developed organically.

The book is divided into many parts by means of a numbering system. These are arranged into a complex system of matrices structured around the number 7. This shows how every remark supports and is supported by the rest. The main remarks are ordered thus:

	a	b	c	d	e	f	g
I	1.1	1.2	2	2.1	2.2	3	3.1
II	2.1	2.2	3	3.1	3.2	3.3	3.4
III	3	3.1	3.2	3.3	3.4	3.5	4
IV	3.2	3.3	3.4	3.5	4	4.1	4.2
V	4	4.1	4.2	4.3	4.4	4.5	5
VI	5	5.1	5.2	5.3	5.4	5.5	5.6
VII	5.6	6	6.1	6.2	6.3	6.4	6.5

Wittgenstein experienced the dehumanizing results of modern, mechanized combat, the ''grand strategies'' of Total War, which engineered the slaughter of millions of men in conditions of unimaginable horror. What effect could such an experience of mass insanity have on a highly sensitive person with an engineer's logical mind?

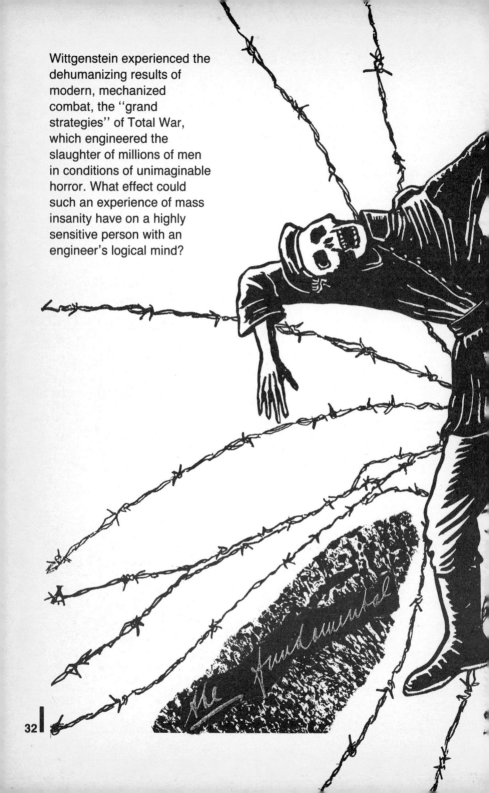

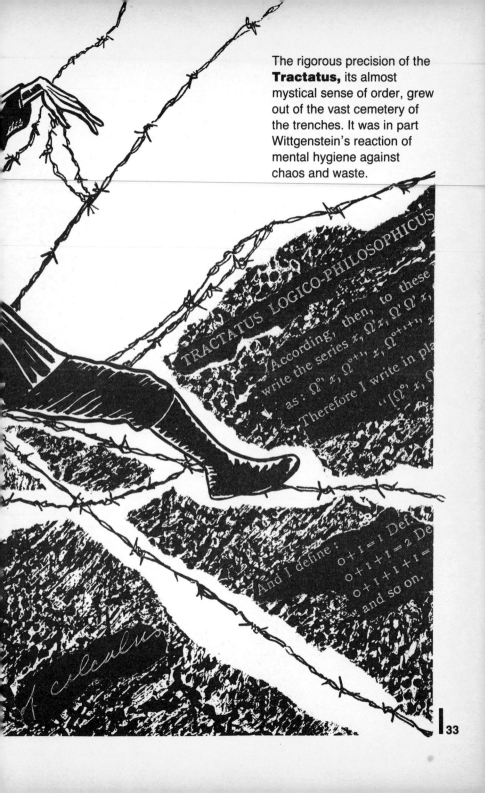

The rigorous precision of the **Tractatus,** its almost mystical sense of order, grew out of the vast cemetery of the trenches. It was in part Wittgenstein's reaction of mental hygiene against chaos and waste.

FACTS ARE <u>NOT</u> THINGS

The book begins by stating how the world is.

The world is the totality of facts, not of things, and it breaks down into independent facts which divide the world up.

With these gnomic words, he is not referring to the world we experience in space or time but to **logical space**.

NOT A FACT

Things, like this chair or that tree, are not independent of their surroundings and so are not facts.

NOT A FACT

Facts are in logical space and independent of one another and can only be stated or asserted.

It is a **fact** that there is a chair in this room.

FACT

FACT

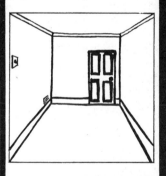

And it is a **fact** that there is not a hippopotamus.

Whereas things exist, are in space and time and have properties such as hardness, colour, etc.

FACTS, PICTURES AND STATES OF AFFAIRS

Now a fact could be otherwise — a hippopotamus might be in the room — so we must be able to grasp possibilities independently of their realization.

We can PICTURE facts to ourselves.

These pictures of facts are mirrored in language to give us meaning, so that we can say truly a hippopotamus **is not** in the room.

For this to be possible the world must consist of simple objects fitting into one another like the links on a chain to form **states of affairs**.

Reality is the existence or non-existence of these states of affairs.

NON-EXISTENTIAL TRUTHS

These insights into the nature of language and the world came early to Wittgenstein. In his first term as an undergraduate Russell reported that: "He maintained, for example, at one time that all existential propositions are meaningless."
This was in a lecture room, and Russell invited him to consider the proposition . . .

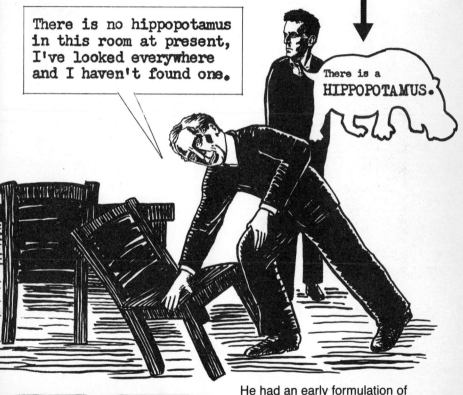

There is no hippopotamus in this room at present, I've looked everywhere and I haven't found one.

There is a HIPPOPOTAMUS.

He had an early formulation of what in the **Tractatus** he saw more clearly — that we can speak of existence only when we assert the truth of some proposition that is not itself existential.

NAMES, OBJECTS AND CONCEPTUAL RELATIONS

Now what is it in language that corresponds to the simple objects linked together that make up the substance of the world?

The elements in propositions are **names** or **simple signs** which combine in determinate ways to represent the way things are.

These "names" are not like ordinary names such as "John" or "Paris".

But the elements or "names" in propositions can only be elucidated in the actual use of language to depict.

The problem is, I can't give any examples of such "names", and you'll see why in a moment.

Ordinary names are understood from within language by means of definitions or descriptions.

It follows that we can only grasp **conceptual relations** by a logical analysis of ordinary sentences which shows how they are determined by combinations derived from simple objects.

So at the deepest level there are two independent moments — the fact of combination and the fact that it is objects that are so combined. All this enables us to get a glimpse of how language can be understood without its being explained to us.

PHILOSOPHY AND SCIENCE

It is vital to see the mysteriousness of this account and how different it is from analysis in natural science. Wittgenstein stressed the difference between philosophy and science.

The purpose of philosophy is the logical clarification of thoughts.

Philosophy is not a teaching but an activity.

A philosophical work consists mainly of elucidations.

The result of philosophy is not "philosophical propositions", but the clarification of propositions. Philosophy should take thoughts that are otherwise turbid and blurred, so to speak, and make them clear and sharp. (**Tractatus** 4.112)

40

The business of philosophy is **critique.** It clarifies the limits of meaningful language. Science on the other hand consists of all true propositions. It studies the existence or non-existence of **states of affairs.**

H_2O

Science works within meaning and language. So, if we ask a chemist what water is made of, he will reply of oxygen and hydrogen, and this can be demonstrated by him.

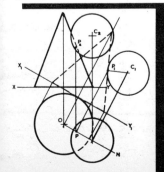

In geometry we can say that a line is constructed from an infinite number of points and many deductions can be made from this.

41

Wittgenstein's analysis is not like the scientist's. He is interested in the limits of meaning and language.

That's why I can't give you examples of "simple objects or names". Names only occur in the CONTEXT OF A PROPOSITION.

A name in this sense is not a tag attached to an object, but is subject to rules of combination with other names. Nor can we point to simple objects, for space and time are **forms** of objects. Objects make up the substance of the world — they contain the possibility of all situations.

So we can't even say that objects exist or don't exist, as they are not facts or things. They are useful in so far as they help us elucidate the nature of propositions. And propositions are important as they throw light on thought.

WHAT IS THOUGHT?

A thought is a logical picture of the facts, and a proposition is the expression of a thought in a way that we can read or hear. So what is a logical picture?

Consider a gramophone record. It consists of variegated grooves on a plastic base. When the record is played, the information contained in the grooves is reproduced in the music.

So the spatial patterns on the record must share a **form** with the auditory relations of the notes in the music. The music, the score of the music, a digital recording of the music and an analog recording all share **homologous form**, but there is no way of representing the form.

Homologous form simply shows itself in its various manifestations. In a similar way, a logical picture depicts the way things are because it shares homologous form with reality.

In other words, you can't **SHOW** a thought.

Let us look more closely at logic. As we have said, a thought is a logical picture; but a picture may be true or false. I can think . . .

NO CONDOR!

A condor is flying over my house...

This is a perfectly logical thought but is not true, because if I look, I see no condor.

So logic is not concerned with whether something is or is not the case but that something **is**, that there is the world and not nothing.

Logic enables us to make true and false statements but does not say anything about what is in the world. It is the great mirror which shows something essential about the world, but cannot say what it is.

Common sense and science, on the other hand, tell us what is in the world.

Two extreme forms of logical proposition are instructive. These are logical contradictions and tautologies.

If I say: "He is a man and not a man," this is a **contradiction**, provided "man" means the same in both parts of the proposition — e.g. the second "man" does not mean "a wimp". But we cannot apply it to the world to see if it is true or false.

If I say: "I know that either it is raining or it is not raining," this is a **tautology**. It is the opposite of a contradiction, in that it is true whatever the circumstances, but it says nothing as it applies to nothing in particular. It is like the Bellman's map in Lewis Carroll's *Hunting of the Snark:* "A perfect and absolute blank".

OSCAR ZARATE

Tautology and contradiction are not really propositions at all, although they appear to be so. They lack sense because they say nothing. They give no information, but are of great importance as they show the nature of logic.

THEY GIVE NO INFORMATION

Wittgenstein argued that all logical propositions can be reduced to tautologies.

Logic shows logical form, but states nothing about what is in the world. It exhibits the world.

MAP

Logical signs speak for themselves. There are no logical objects.

Ordinary propositions, on the other hand, show how things stand, if they are true, and say that they do indeed stand that way.

THE PROBLEM OF THE SELF

Solipsism is the belief that oneself is the only real object of knowledge or the only thing that really exists.

You know, there's a germ of truth in it.

Is there? Consider the lady who wrote to me, saying she was a solipsist but was suprised there weren't more of them!

H'm!

It is clearly nonsense to be persuaded by someone that he or she alone exists, or to argue to others (or even oneself) that oneself alone exists.

But who is this "self" that the solipsist believes exists alone in the world?

We can use the analogy of vision.

We say "I see a cherry tree" but can we see the "I" that sees the cherry tree?

I look in a mirror. I can see my eyes but can I see the "I" that sees them?

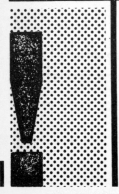

Now think a thought. Can you find a thinker apart from a thought? I can "think" of a thinker apart from a thought, but if I think harder, I realize that this is just another thought that I am thinking.

NO SELF

THERE IS NO **I**

There is no "I", no ego or subject, that stands alone in the world and sees and thinks and confers sense on what it sees and thinks. But there is a language of thought, and "I" is the formal point of reference for it.

So I am in order when I say, "I think".
The subject cannot be found in the world,
yet "I" have lots of experiences in the world.

What I experience is MY experience. That is the truth of solipsism, but this does not mean that it is my possession, for there is no subject to possess it.

THIS IS NOT AN EYE

I and the world coincide, and yet my world is unique.

I am the limit of the world, but I cannot draw a boundary round it, for to do that I would have to be able to step outside it, which I cannot do.

ETHICS

According to the analysis of the **Tractatus**, the world is wholly contingent. It is an aggregate of mutually independent states of affairs. What we experience as links between events, the "causal nexus", is superstition.

← "contingent"–uncertain, incidental, conditional

Causality is not a law which nature obeys, but the form in which the propositions of science are cast.

OSCAR ZARATE

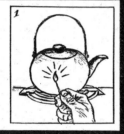

There is no compulsion making one thing happen because another has happened. The only necessity that exists is *logical* necessity. The whole modern conception of the world is founded on the illusion that the so-called laws of nature are the explanations of natural phenomena. (**Tractatus** 6.37-.371)

In fact, ancient people who believed in the gods and in Fate were clearer than we moderns, as they had a clear and acknowledged terminus, whereas we believe that EVERYTHING is explainable.

So where do we find meaning and happiness in a wholly contingent world?

51

WHAT IS HAPPINESS?

When one sees the world rightly, one understands that there is no "psychological self" which thinks, believes or feels. Psychological states are altogether part of the world, in so far as they are describable. They are bare facts — the fact that I am thinking such and such, or that I am feeling such and such, etc.

But happiness is not a state of mind. It is not the same as "feeling good", nor is it a judgement or reflection. So there are no physical or psychological criteria to distinguish between happiness and unhappiness. It depends on my realizing the limits of the **sense** of the world, and not on any facts.

The world of the happy man is a different one from that of the unhappy man.

The world is my world, and the way I live determines its structure and may enable me to see it correctly, that is, as a limited whole.

So happiness is no more a concern of psychology than of physics or palaeontology.

Psychology is on the same level as the other sciences because its propositions, like theirs, are all equally descriptive of what is or is not the case.
This is in marked opposition to common Western beliefs in the 20th century, in which therapies based on psychology are supposed to lead to happiness.

JOSEPHINE KING

Since what can be said is limited to the existence or non-existence of states of affairs, which are without exception contingent, then ethical propositions like logical ones lack sense. They **show** but cannot **say**.

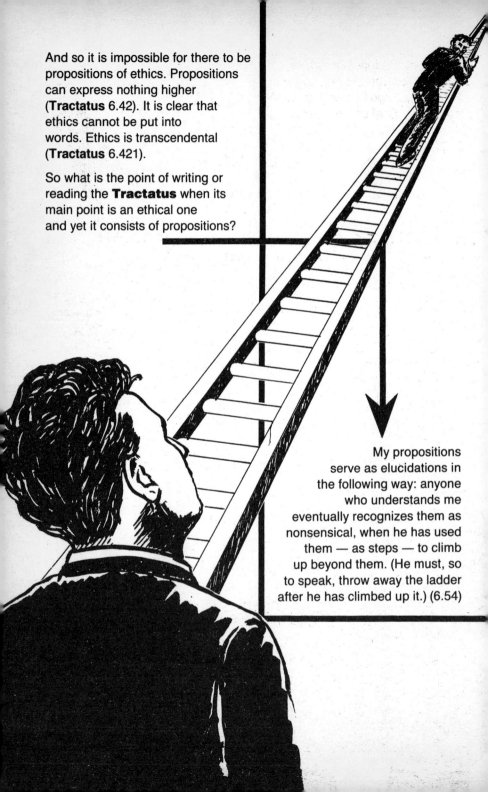

And so it is impossible for there to be propositions of ethics. Propositions can express nothing higher (**Tractatus** 6.42). It is clear that ethics cannot be put into words. Ethics is transcendental (**Tractatus** 6.421).

So what is the point of writing or reading the **Tractatus** when its main point is an ethical one and yet it consists of propositions?

My propositions serve as elucidations in the following way: anyone who understands me eventually recognizes them as nonsensical, when he has used them — as steps — to climb up beyond them. (He must, so to speak, throw away the ladder after he has climbed up it.) (6.54)

Wittgenstein clarified his ethics
in a lecture given in 1929.
He distinguished between the **relative**
and the **ethical** use of "good".

If I play tennis badly and I'm criticized for it, I can reply, "Yes, but I'm content to play badly."

But if I'm a chronic liar and satisfied to be one, most people would say...

Lies! That's not good enough — you OUGHT not to be satisfied!

But this "ought" cannot be translated into a statement of fact. For example, I could always find reasons to continue lying. So this "ought" points to an **absolute**. There can be no science or theory of ethics, it cannot be taught or explained. 55

If a man could write a book on Ethics which
really was a book on Ethics, this book would,
with an explosion, destroy all the other
books in the world.

However, we can try to elucidate absolute value. Wittgenstein gestures towards the limits of language in three different ways.

At sheer **EXISTENCE** ◄

the experience of
being astonished
before the existence
of the world

At the **SUBJECT** ◄

the experience of
feeling absolutely
safe no matter
what happens

And at **ETHICS** ◄

the experience of
feeling guilty,
in the sense of
falling short of
some absolute
requirement which
we could not specify.

These are all experiences and so are **facts**. But it is nonsensical to speak of them, as they refer to situations which cannot exist in the world. We cannot be absolutely safe, for example.

A fact cannot contain any absolute value. Yet, for some, these experiences seem to point beyond themselves, while others may appeal to different experiences whose theme is the sublime.

We cannot **describe** the limits of language and the world or point them out to someone. Nor can we do this to ourselves.

We have to walk our own path and knock our heads against senseless propositions, before we can understand the world as a limited whole.

No amount of reading can do this for us. So the first sentence of the preface to the **Tractatus** reads: "Perhaps this book will be understood only by someone who has himself already had the thoughts expressed in it — or at least similar thoughts."

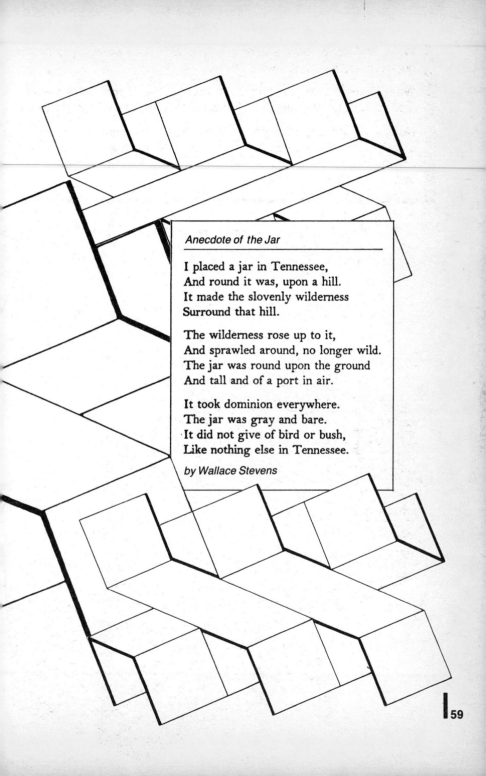

Anecdote of the Jar

I placed a jar in Tennessee,
And round it was, upon a hill.
It made the slovenly wilderness
Surround that hill.

The wilderness rose up to it,
And sprawled around, no longer wild.
The jar was round upon the ground
And tall and of a port in air.

It took dominion everywhere.
The jar was gray and bare.
It did not give of bird or bush,
Like nothing else in Tennessee.

by Wallace Stevens

After the war, Wittgenstein found himself one of the wealthiest men in Austria due to his father's astuteness in putting the family's wealth into American bonds.

I'm giving it all to my brother and sisters. I want to live only on the money I earn.

He moved out of his family home and took lodgings near the Teacher's Training College, where he was trained as an elementary school teacher.

Since the TRACTATUS has solved all the problems of philosophy, I'm going to work as a school teacher.

He now wanted to live and work amongst the rural poor; a meagre income but a rich inner life were the ideals he sought to live by and teach.

He was a born teacher, although an unorthodox one. He did not lecture but led the children on by means of questions.

He had them inventing a steam engine, learning anatomy by assembling the skeleton of a cat, astronomy by observing the night sky and so on.

He put great emphasis on mathematics and taught it to a higher level than was expected of the age group.

He taught in village schools south of Vienna.
But he was not popular with the villagers.

He was prone to pull a girl's hair if she
could not grasp the basics of algebra!

He wrote to Russell . . .

So he moved on and taught in other village schools, getting much the same reaction from the local people.

During this time he wrote a spelling dictionary for use in elementary schools which enjoyed a limited success.

In 1926, he gave up teaching — to the relief of the villagers, but to the regret of the District School Inspectors who placed great value on his ability as a teacher.

A PERFECT HOUSE

From 1926-28, he was involved in designing and building a house in Vienna for his sister Gretl. He was a passionate admirer of Adolf Loos (1870-1933), the modernist Viennese architect.

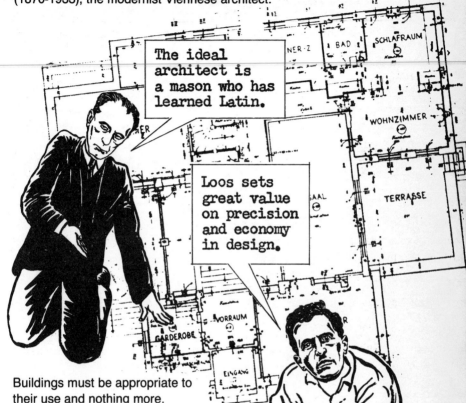

The ideal architect is a mason who has learned Latin.

Loos sets great value on precision and economy in design.

Buildings must be appropriate to their use and nothing more.
His architecture was designed to show in the modern its relationship to the classical.
Wittgenstein's house on the Kundmanngasse is austerely monumental. Clarity, rigour and precision characterize it.
He was meticulous in its construction; thus when it was nearly finished, he had the ceiling of one big room raised by three centimetres to get the proportions exactly right.

It now serves as the home for the Cultural Department of the Bulgarian Embassy.

FALLING IN LOVE?

Building the house got Wittgenstein involved in Viennese society. He fell in love with a Swiss girl called Marguerite, who was a friend of his sister Gretl.

She was much younger than he and was a lively, artistic girl from a wealthy family with no interest in philosophy.

Going out with him is an adventure! He doesn't dress respectably — look at him, worn out jacket, open neck shirt, heavy boots!

Yes, and I'll only eat at cheap cafés.

They saw much of one another for some years and Wittgenstein wanted to marry her.

In 1931, she went with him to his house in Norway.

He spent most of the time praying and meditating and left me alone.

She left after two weeks, having decided that she had better not marry him! They remained friends, however.

A FLAW IN WITTGENSTEIN'S LOGIC

During Wittgenstein's school-teaching career, he had occasional contact with philosophers who were interested in the **Tractatus**, but after 1928 he began to see some fundamental flaws in it.

One of the main influences on this change of view was Piero Sraffa, a Marxist economist and close friend of Antonio Gramsci (1891-1937), the imprisoned Italian Communist leader.

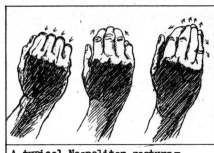

A typical Neapolitan gesture – brushing the chin with fingertips – which conveys insult.

A proposition and what it describes MUST have some logical form.

Oh yes? And what's the logical form of this?

Sraffa, with his Marxist emphasis on the essentially social and interactive nature of language, had a lasting and profound influence on Wittgenstein.

THE VIENNA CIRCLE

In 1927, Wittgenstein began to have meetings with some members of the Vienna Circle. This was a group of philosophers, mathematicians and scientists, led by Moritz Schlick (1882-1936), a philosopher who was assassinated by a Nazi student.

If you believe that, you've completely misunderstood the TRACTATUS! It's an exploration of the ethical, the limits of language and of thought — that's what it's about.

Like you, we believe philosophy should be scientific.

They regarded Wittgenstein and the **Tractatus** with awesome reverence.

ERÖFFENTLICHUNGEN DES EREINES ERNST MACH

ENSCHAFTLICHE AUFFASSUNG

WIENER KREIS

VEREIN ERNST MACH
PREIS S 2.— (RM 1.20)

ERLAG / WIEN

Rudolf Carnap (1891-1970), one of the Circle's distinguished philosophers, described Wittgenstein's way of philosophizing very well.

"His point of view and his attitude towards people and problems, even theoretical problems, were much more similar to those of a creative artist than to those of a scientist; one might almost say, similar to those of a religious prophet or a seer. When he started to formulate his view on some specific philosophical problem, we often felt the internal struggle that occurred in him at that very moment, a struggle by which he tried to penetrate from darkness to light under an intense and painful strain, which was even visible on his most expressive face. When finally, sometimes after a prolonged arduous effort, his answer came forth, his statement stood before us like a newly created piece of art or a divine revelation. Not that he asserted his views dogmatically . . . But the impression he made on us was as if insight came to him as through a divine inspiration, so that we could not help feeling that any sober rational comment or analysis of it would be a profanation."

In 1929, Wittgenstein returned to Cambridge. Keynes, who had been encouraging him to return, wrote to his wife. "Well, God has arrived. I met him on the 5.15 train."

But he had no money and no degree. So it was decided that he put the **Tractatus** forward for a Ph.D.

His old friends Moore, now the Professor of Philosophy, and Russell were the examiners. The exam was a farce, ending with Wittgenstein clapping each of his examiners on the shoulder consolingly.

He was awarded his degree and got a five-year fellowship at Trinity College.

HOW DID WITTGENSTEIN TEACH?

His way of teaching was unique. He did not give formal lectures, but would think out loud before a small group of students in his college rooms.

I never use notes — thoughts become stale that way.

These meetings are unnerving and confrontational.

Often he'll just sit there, cursing at his own stupidity.

Long periods of silence were frequent.

Sometimes the meetings would be dialogues with various people present. But he would be uncompromising both to himself and others, and people felt they were in the presence of extreme seriousness and depth of thought.

His attitude to academic life was ambivalent. He hated the stiffness, artificiality and self-satisfaction of the university. He wrote to a friend, "What I miss most is someone I can talk nonsense to by the yard." His letters to friends are full of jokes and nonsense.

I strongly advise you against becoming academic philosophers. The temptation to fake thinking amongst them is very great.

Good thoughts rather than clever ones are what he valued.

When told that there was to be the annual jamboree for academic philosophers in Cambridge in 1947, he said it was as if he had been told that there would be bubonic plague in Cambridge, and he would make sure he was in London — which he was!

FALLING IN LOVE AGAIN

Soon after becoming a lecturer, Wittgenstein fell in love with a young Trinity undergraduate, Francis Skinner, who became his constant companion and valued collaborator in philosophical work.

Skinner, the most promising mathematician of his year, was a rather shy, good-looking and very gentle young man who was clearly destined for an academic career.

Under Ludwig's influence, I gave up university and became a factory mechanic.

When he died of polio in 1941, I felt guilty for a long time after. I had unfaithful thoughts about him in the last two years of his life.

But in 1946 Wittgenstein fell in love with Ben Richards, an undergraduate student of medicine at Cambridge who was nearly forty years younger than him; this relationship brought him great joy and continued until his death.

In 1947, he resigned from his professorship at Cambridge because he wanted to write and because he felt his teaching did not have a good effect.

> All that students want from me is a clever formula or theory – and that's not important!

So he went to live in Ireland, away from the "disintegrating and putrefying English civilization".

Much of the time he lived in a little cottage on the west coast of Ireland at the mouth of the Killary harbour. There he wrote some of his most important work.

In 1949, he went to stay with his former student and friend Norman Malcolm at Cornell University in the U.S. He took part in meetings with graduate students. His presence had a tremendous impact.

A witness described how Malcolm appeared and . . .

"On his arm leaned a slight, older man, dressed in windjacket and old army trousers. If it had not been for his face, alight with intelligence, one might have taken him for some vagabond Malcolm had found along the road and decided to bring out of the cold."

When his name was mentioned "a loud and instantaneous gasp went up from the assembled students".

Soon after this, he became ill and returned to England and was diagnosed as suffering from cancer of the prostate. The last two years of his life were spent between Vienna, Oxford and Cambridge, staying with friends and family.

He continued to do significant work in philosophy until the day before he finally lost consciousness.

He died at Cambridge in April 1951.

PERSONALITY

Much has been written on Wittgenstein's personality — which he would have hated.

He was an imposing figure, and one finds again and again his friends, family and students saying he was "a true genius", "the most independent spirit", "fearless", "the least neurotic of men", that he possessed "an intensity of concentration that impressed itself on one as disinterestedness", and so on.

People tended to be fascinated or repelled by him, as he was very direct in his approach to people and was impatient of any pretentiousness.

- He was about five feet six inches tall, and slender. As a young man, he was handsome and immaculately dressed, but when older dressed simply with no tie and shirt open at the neck.
- The magic of his personality and style was infectious and pupils tended to imitate him. This caused him much pain as he valued independent thinking above all.
- He was a deeply serious man and put his soul into everything he did.
- He was not learned or widely read, but would only read what he could wholeheartedly assimilate. He tended to read his favourite books over and over again.
- He was very fond of "hard-boiled" American detective stories, claiming that there was more philosophy in them than in academic philosophy journals.
- He was not religious in the conventional sense, but had a deep respect for some religious authors — Augustine, Kierkegaard and the Bible come to mind.
- For him, everything depended on the spirit in which something is done. This was true for his way of teaching, attitude to cooking and attitude to friends.
- Knowledge was intimately connected with doing.
- He could design a house, make a sculpture, or conduct an orchestra.
- He was an engineer by training and was never at loggerheads with machines.
- Music was central to his life.
- He had a phenomenal talent for whistling and could whistle complicated parts from Classical music.
- The music of Bach, Beethoven, Schubert and Schumann were amongst his favourites.
- He had no interest in modern music.
- His outlook was typically one of gloom.
- He intensely disliked academic life.
- He always avoided any publicity and regarded the Press as one of the disasters of modern life.
- Modern times to him were a dark age.
- The idols of progress and the belief that technology will solve all our problems, he felt were profoundly wrong.
- Only a change in our way of life would heal the sickness of our age — and this is only likely to happen when disaster confronts us.

His intensity and capacity to judge show in his quick responses and critical aptness.

Thus, when told that someone was working on a thesis as to why the League of Nations had failed...

"Tell him to find out first why wolves eat lambs!"

On being told that someone had given up working on his PhD, as he had decided he had nothing original to say...

"For that action alone they should give him his PhD."

When someone was talking about progress in history...

"With all the ugly sides of our civilization, I am sure I would rather live as we do now than have to live as the caveman did."

"Yes, of course you would. But would the caveman?"

His writings are full of apt pictures and analogies.

AFTER THE TRACTATUS

There are some 20 titles of writings by Wittgenstein in English, but only the **Tractatus** and two short pieces were actually published with his approval. The majority are remarks extracted from his notebooks by various editors, some of his lectures and conversations put together from notes by his students, and some letters — all of course published after his death.

He constantly changed his text, reformulating his remarks, putting them in different contexts to test their meaning.

When he reached a conclusion he would often start all over again, re-exploring the topic from a different point of view. It was as if he wanted to keep everything in flux, to show work in progress rather than grand philosophical conclusions.

I should not like my writing to spare other people the trouble of thinking. But, if possible, to stimulate someone to thoughts of his own.

(Preface to **Philosophical Investigations**)

PHILOSOPHICAL INVESTIGATIONS

His best known book is the **Philosophical Investigations** which was published two years after his death. The first two thirds of the remarks were chosen and put in order by him.

It is a carefully crafted book which concerns many subjects: "the concepts of meaning, of understanding, of a proposition, of logic, the foundations of mathematics, states of consciousness, and other things".

It is written, like the **Tractatus**, as a series of remarks, but they tend to be longer and less aphoristic than in the early work.

Some are also in the form of dialogues with an alter ego who voices a variety of positions.

There are many images, some satire, and how-to instructions.

It is easier to read than the **Tractatus**, as it has no logical symbols, but its ease is deceptive.

WHAT IS PHILOSOPHY?

Wittgenstein was always interested in the nature of philosophy, and from the 1930s on he became clear that philosophy was a

THERAPY

– a very ancient view of it, for Socrates and many ancient Greek philosophers practised it that way.

The aim of philosophy is: "Thoughts that are at peace".

We are not at peace with ourselves or others because we are entrenched in **habits of thought** connected with "the way people live".

He saw that there is a clear connection between language and ways of life.

> Our way of life is mirrored in language.

OSCAR ZARATE

"Human beings are profoundly enmeshed in philosophical — i.e. grammatical confusions. They cannot be freed without first being extricated from the extraordinary variety of associations which hold them prisoner. You have as it were to reconstitute their entire language. — But this language grew up as it did because human beings had — and have — the tendency to think in that way."

85

THERAPY BY INVESTIGATION

The trouble with the **Tractatus** was that it had tried to penetrate things.

It was as if the essence of things was hidden from us, and we had, by means of analysis, to dig out what lay within it.

It then claimed to have found "unassailable and definitive" truths and "the final solution of the problems".

My new therapy simply puts everything before us, and neither explains nor deduces anything. — Since everything lies open to view there is nothing to explain. For what is hidden, for example, is of no interest to us...

The work of the philosopher consists in assembling **reminders** for a particular purpose. Philosophy is simply the particular individual worries that are called "philosophical problems" — but are not the ones often recognized by academic philosophy.

The aspect of things that are most important to us are hidden because of their SIMPLICITY and FAMILIARITY.

A common-sense person, when he reads earlier philosophers, thinks — quite rightly — "Sheer nonsense". When he listens to me, he thinks — quite rightly again — "Nothing but stale truisms". That is how the image of philosophy has changed. (MS 219, 6)

TAKING FOR GRANTED . . .

Wittgenstein's later philosophy is not tentative in the way a scientist might be in presenting his results. Instead, he thinks his way through the **taken-for-granted** forms of everyday speech.

I do this to immerse myself in the waters of doubt to renew my power to think.

It is this immersion that can free us from ingrained habits of thought. He wants to get a clear view of what troubles us.

A philosophical problem has the form: "I don't know my way about".

He acts as a guide, getting us to look at the actual landscape we are walking over, rather than having our head buried in a map.

That is why, when he actually gets us to look, we have to agree with him.

THE METHOD

So what is Wittgenstein's method of therapy?
He is not concerned with **arguments** to
establish a position, as in much traditional
philosophy.

Rather, he is teaching a skill that is critical and
destabilizing, seeking to fracture the artificial
unities we construct with our minds, so that we
can see differences.

I'd like to
use as a motto,
"I'll teach you
differences",
from Shakespeare's
KING LEAR.

"There is not **a** philosophical
method, though there are indeed
methods, like different therapies."
(**PI** 133)

The therapy must be appropriate to
the persons involved and the problem.

In contrast to psychological therapies, Wittgenstein's therapy does not depend on any **theory** of the mind.

I do not seek to explain things by "cognitive processes", "instincts" or "mental mechanisms".

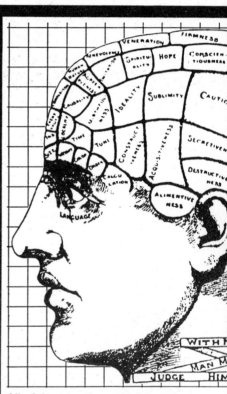

All of these notions tend to make the problem subservient to the theory, as the theorist tends to see the problem through the spectacles of his theory.

"We must do away with all explanation and allow only description in its place". (**PI** 109)

THE HYPNOTISM OF LANGUAGE

Language is a poison that can be used to seduce, mislead and bewitch us, but it can also heal, as when we speak truly.

The ambiguous nature of language is central to Wittgenstein's thought.

Philosophy is a battle against the bewitchment of our intelligence by means of language.

When we are bewitched, we tend to stare — the hypnotic gaze.

We then tend to see illusory "essences" which rise out of pictures embedded in language, but which seem to lie deep in the mind or the world.

Distinctions and differences are missed, the eye is "dazzled by the ideal". (**PI** 100)

We try to grasp the ideal or dig it out of the depths. Somehow we feel compelled to penetrate the phenomena.

All this leads us to talking disguised nonsense.

THE THERAPY OF ILLUSION – DESCRIPTION

So in opposition to these compulsions, Wittgenstein encourages us to describe by following the **play** of language.

What he calls "depth grammar" is not something that lies beneath appearance, like the unconscious in psychoanalysis.

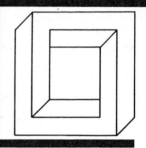

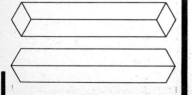

It is discovered in the subtle articulations of appearance within language itself. It allows us to make the difference between sense and nonsense.

So Wittgenstein **describes**.

- He may describe the pictures that hypnotize us and get us to see their lack of application.

- He may invite us to remember how we would teach a child to use a word or phrase.

- Or get us to see differences in the use of expressions and their connecting links.

- Or invent new uses of words, sometimes absurd ones, to help loosen the grip of the customary forms of language.

This triangle

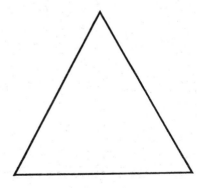

can be seen as
a triangular hole,
as a solid,
as a geometrical drawing,
as standing on its base,
as hanging from its apex,
as a mountain,
as a wedge,
as an arrow or pointer,
as an overturned object
which is meant to stand on
the shorter side of the
right angle,
as a half parallelogram,
and as various other things.
(PI p.200)

It seems we see it as an interpretation. But is it possible to SEE according to an INTERPRETATION?

Thinking is at the heart of human life — and something that philosophers are supposed to be particularly good at.

Logic is sometimes said to be the **science of thinking** and Wittgenstein was particularly interested in it.

So Wittgenstein's approach to thought is important and illustrates his method well.

Thought appears simple until we reflect upon it.

Reflection brings obscurity — which is the result of the shadow cast by the inquirer himself.

What is it to think?

Well, at first sight we all seem to know what it is. If asked: "What do you think of so and so, or such and such?", we can all answer, provided we are familiar with the person or subject.

We readily say: "I think it is going to rain" or "I think I will take two weeks holiday".

And if we see someone playing a good game of chess or making a complicated calculation, we know that they **must** be thinking.

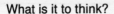

There are some complications. Most of us would say that monkeys, dogs and cats think, but not so well as us. But do flies think or live sponges? When do babies start thinking? In the womb? At birth? And how do we decide?

"**Thinking**, a widely ramified concept. A concept that comprises many manifestations of life. The *phenomena* of thinking are widely scattered."

Now compare these different ways of thinking.

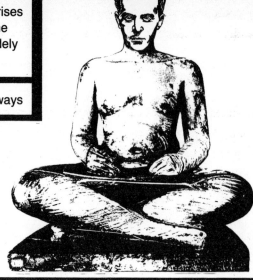

▶ speak thoughtfully;

▶ speak without thought;

▶ think before speaking;

▶ speak before thinking;

▶ think while speaking;

▶ speak to yourself in imagination;

▶ think of someone;

▶ think of a solution to a puzzle;

▶ let a thought cross your mind;

▶ whistle a tune thoughtfully and then without thought;

▶ now just be thoughtful.

The word "thought" is a simple everyday word and appears to correspond to a simple activity, but when we try it out in different situations we see it is ragged. We had a false picture of it.

Because it is ONE WORD, we think it represents one sort of activity.

DIRECTOR

We forgot that a word's meaning depends on its staging, the scene or circumstances in which it is used.

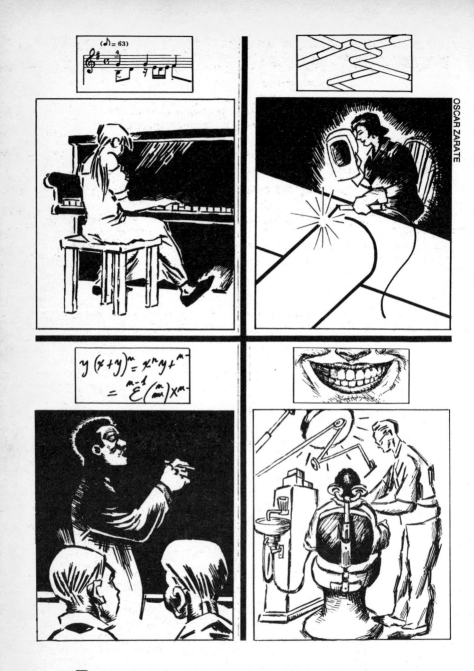

One learns the word "think" – its use –
under certain circumstances, which, however,
ONE DOES NOT LEARN TO DESCRIBE.

So let's think about thinking!

Is it an activity?

We talk of "running hard", and running is definitely an activity.

We were told at school to "think harder".

So what did we **do** then?

If we frown and look solemn, does that mean we are thinking *harder*?

at is the difference between *trying hard to run faster*
trying hard to think?

stly activity that we cannot see
ind?

There is a great temptation to imagine we can actually look into our minds and watch ourselves while we think. What we observe will be what the word means!

We imagine that we can inwardly point or look (by introspection), as if we had some sort of "inner space" where inner activities occurred that could be named.

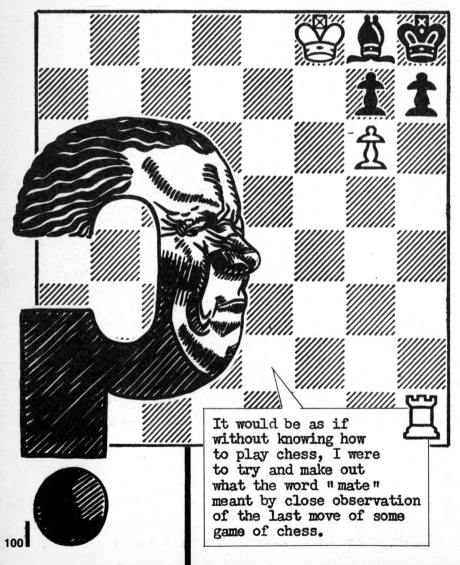

It would be as if without knowing how to play chess, I were to try and make out what the word "mate" meant by close observation of the last move of some game of chess.

In other words, to understand **thought**, we need to understand the rules for the **use** of the word "think".

Instead, we are hypnotized by the idea of the mind as working in an invisible space in which we can "see" or infer that thinking is going on.

Can we use the little word "this" to point to thinking, and so say "*This* is thinking", as we certainly can to running?

We can observe activities and say "This is running", or infer processes and say "This is particle spin", as in physics.

But we can't meaningfully say "This is thinking" in the same sense.

Supposing two people are asked to find the square root of a number.

One strides up and down, frowns, holds his head in his hands, and comes up with the wrong result.

The other pauses a moment and answers correctly.

The first has thought hard? We could say so, but we could also say he did not think much at all. Striding up and down is **not** thinking.

Nothing **need** go on when we think — neither bodily gestures nor interior monologue nor mental images.

The first person may have said lots of things to himself, and had lots of images, but that does not mean he was finding the square root.

The various accompaniments of finding the square root are not the same as finding it. **It is finding it that is the mark of thought.**

We do not look inside our minds to see if we are thoughtful. What matters is whether we hit the nail on the head.

103

LANGUAGE AND THOUGHT

Sometimes we are asked: "So what did you think?" And we then report what we thought: "I thought this and then that etc." Here we are *expressing* what we thought in an ordered way.

Ouch!

Misleading parallel: the expression of pain is a cry — the expression of thought, a proposition.

We may feel a pain and cry out. But do we think a thought inside our minds and then say it?

Of course, we can keep our thoughts to ourselves.

But can we think a thought internally **without language** and then report it?

If this were so, it would imply there are two processes — **language** and **thoughts**.

But can you isolate thought from language when you speak thoughtfully?

Can we inwardly **see** our thoughts, as we can feel a pain without groaning?

We do not report what we thought by observing a process, but by thinking, and then perhaps voicing the thought.

There is not a mental process which we then see as a thought.

I'll take a holiday.

Nothing needs to be in my consciousness when I think.

If I think to myself: "I will take a holiday in August," the thought carries its own meaning and does not need any further accompaniment in my mind.

REPORTING A THOUGHT

A thought may occur in a flash, but the report of it cannot.

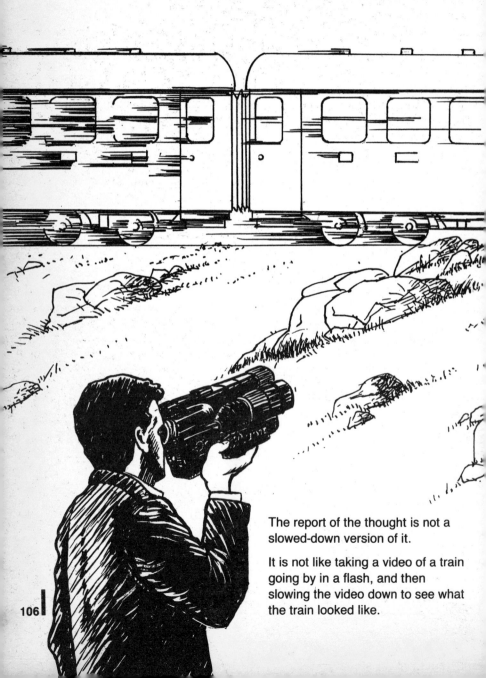

The report of the thought is not a slowed-down version of it.

It is not like taking a video of a train going by in a flash, and then slowing the video down to see what the train looked like.

Thoughts do not go by in parts like the carriages of a train. We think them.

We can have half a train but not half a thought — but we may be half way through expressing a thought or may not have worked out all its implications.

When thoughts occur in a flash, it means we suddenly see what to do or say, rather than something happening suddenly inside us.

The concept of thinking is not the concept of an experience. A thought is more a pointer than a product.

Many people when they "think" get headaches,
because they "think" with their heads.

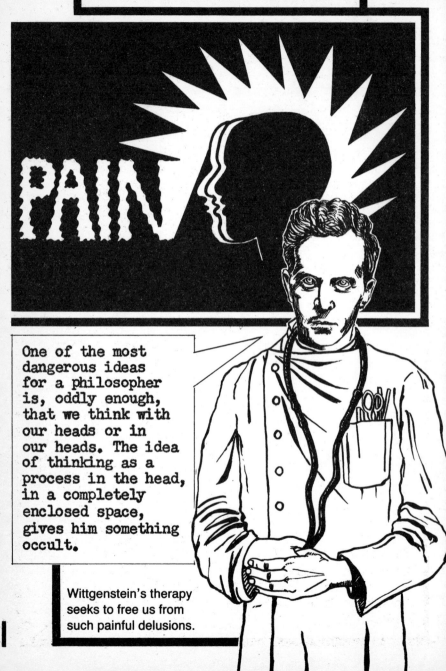

PAIN

One of the most
dangerous ideas
for a philosopher
is, oddly enough,
that we think with
our heads or in
our heads. The idea
of thinking as a
process in the head,
in a completely
enclosed space,
gives him something
occult.

Wittgenstein's therapy
seeks to free us from
such painful delusions.

It is commonly assumed not only that we think with our heads, but that we use language to communicate from our brain or head to other people's.

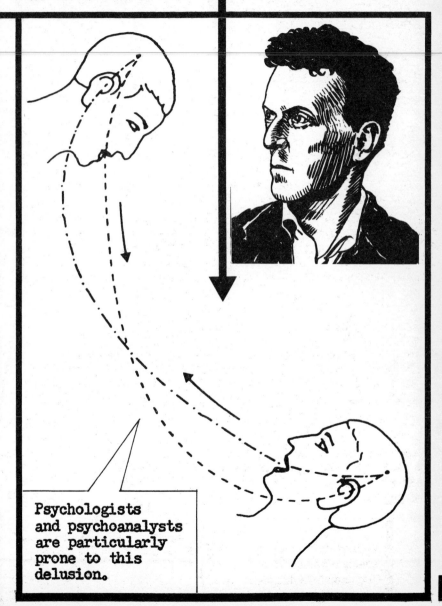

Psychologists and psychoanalysts are particularly prone to this delusion.

We have seen that we cannot isolate thought from what it accompanies.

There are no pure thought processes.

It is not an inner process which we communicate by means of language.

What I think is no more *in* my head than the facts that make it true are *in* the world.

My chair is in the world, but the fact that it is **my** chair is not — it is not anywhere.

Similarly, when I think "This is my chair", the thought is not **in me,** although it is my thought.
So when I tell you what I think, I am not transferring thoughts to you. I do not lose them when I tell them. I express what I think, and for you to understand, you need not think what I think, or have the same thought as I. You may need to know what I think and to say it, but not to have the thought or think it.

LANGUAGE GAMES

The **Philosophical Investigations** starts by describing some simple situations involving the use of words.

For example, purchasing five red apples...

Workmen at a building site giving and receiving orders to bring a slab.

These are examples of language games, which is a notion central to Wittgenstein's thought after 1930.

Language games highlight features of the use of language which we tend to ignore.

They are useful, as they are surveyable. They extend the concepts of language and grammar to include elements that are usually regarded as extraneous.

Language depends on many **non-linguistic** features, above all on human nature.

For example we could not understand the language game of telling a joke unless we had a sense of humour. In addition most humour requires familiarity with the person telling the joke.

Or consider the language we use in connection with death.

If the death of a fellow human mattered no more to us than the death of a fly, then we would not be able to understand the rituals and language of mourning.

CAN WE STAND OUTSIDE LANGUAGE?

When we "think" about language, we are liable to imagine that we can stand **outside** of it.

Thus, it is commonly thought that there is language on one side — in us, so to speak — and reality on the other, outside us.

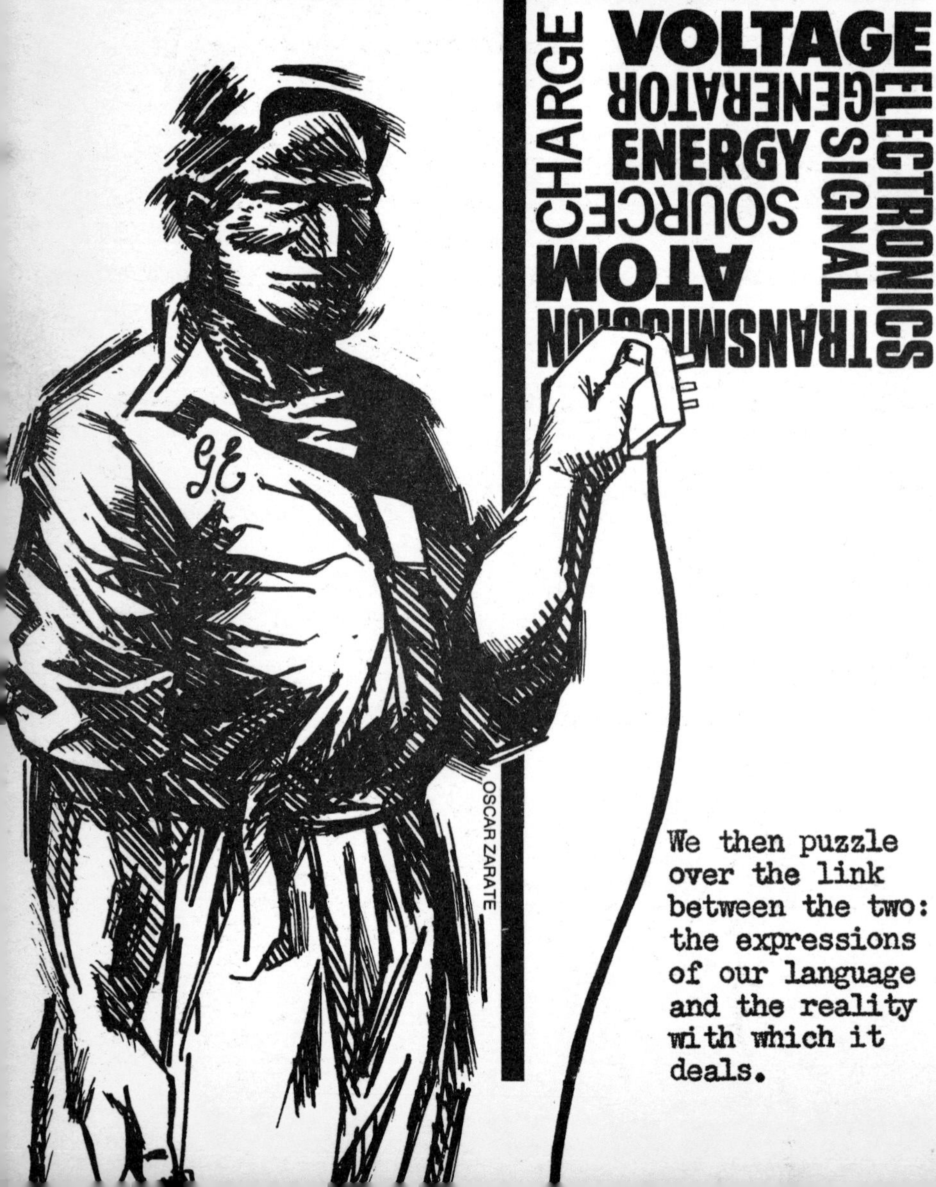

CHARGE

VOLTAGE

GENERATOR

ENERGY

SOURCE

ELECTRONICS

SIGNAL

ATOM

TRANSMISSION

OSCAR ZARATE

We then puzzle over the link between the two: the expressions of our language and the reality with which it deals.

So people have often thought that learning language consists in a series of acquisitions of sundry names for different entities.

POMME
MELA
APFEL
MANZANA

CHAISE
SEDIA
STUHL
SILLA

THIS is a chair, THAT is called red and so on; rather like we acquire the elementary words of a foreign language.

CLEF
CHIAVE
SCHLUSSEL
LLAVE

115

POINTING

In this picture of the way we learn language, it is **pointing** and the words "this" and "that" that make the connection between word and meaning.

Pointing would then be the fundamental form of explanation linking words to the world.

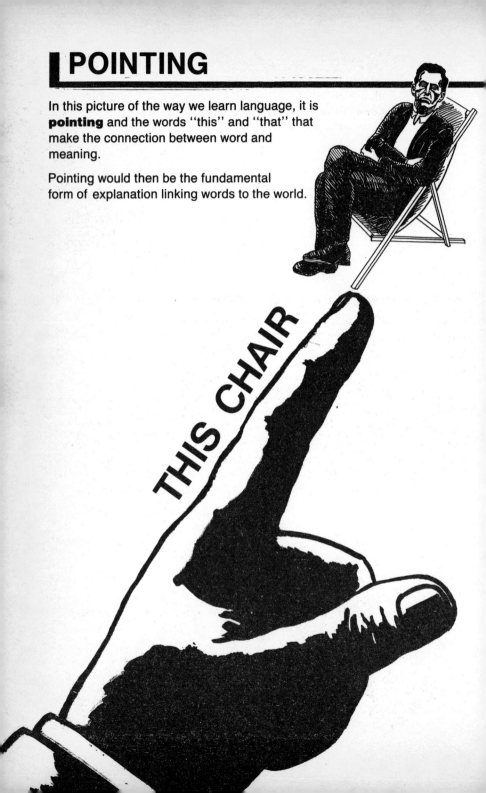

THIS CHAIR

But the gesture of pointing, the words "this" and "that", and the object pointed at, are all part of the language game of explaining meaning, and all require rules for use.

The object pointed at is being used as a sample of what counts as the correct application of a name.

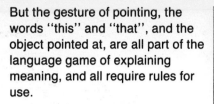

Look, this is a rabbit — or is it a duck?

The words and gestures are not outside of language, and so can't be the explanation for the link between language and reality.

If we see a statue of a man on a horse, lifting his sword and pointing with his left hand, we don't try to figure out what he is pointing at in the surroundings of the statue.

Here we play a different language game. A statue pointing has a different meaning than in "pointing out" the English for certain objects to a foreigner.

Pointing does not link language to the world by fixing meaning.

The gestures of the hand are organs of language.

Persons, bodies and minds inhabit language.

The whole idea of "connections" between language and reality is a **false** one.

Language is self-contained. We can't step out of it.

When we think language is on one side and reality is on the other, and then puzzle as to how they link up, we forget that we dwell in language and are merely imagining that we can point at them.

OUR ORIGINS

Most of us wonder about our origins.

There have been two apparently contradictory accounts of it.

There is the account in Genesis of how God created heaven and earth and all living things in six days.

And there is Darwin's account of how things evolved over enormously long periods, the mechanism of which is genetic variation and natural selection.

To many there is a hopeless contradiction between these two accounts.

The notion of language games helps us here, for it focuses on **action** rather than truth and falsehood.

We *use* the terms "true" and "false" in certain contexts.

Chiefly, when we are investigating whether something is so or not, as in a scientific investigation.

Darwin was imbued with the methods of science: observing, sorting the true from the false; using the methods of scientific inquiry to give an account of the origin of things.

But why can't there be other ways of accounting for the origin of things, using other language games, ones that focus on other practices than dividing truth from falsehood?

A person for whom the practices of worship and prayer are central to his or her life might respond to fundamental questions in a different way and might find the account of origins in Genesis more real.

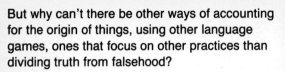

His search would be conducted differently from a scientist's. He might pray for guidance. This would not necessarily produce an answer in the scientific sense, for he would be seeking different satisfactions.

So there need be no contradiction between Genesis and Darwin, but what is important is to be clear on the nature of one's commitment.

Wittgenstein was deeply critical of modern man's lack of self-knowledge, our lack of awareness of our particular commitments. Thus we tend to see the practices of non-literate people as "primitive" and that we are more "evolved" than them.

Take magic. We tend to see it as a pseudo-science trying to do what science does, but badly.

We assume it seeks explanations for natural phenomena and that these are simply wrong.

Magic seeks different satisfactions from science. It is best seen as a highly developed gesture language, not depending on hypotheses or evidence, or seeking causal explanations as does science.

So there is no progress in magic as there is in science.

> If someone is love-sick, a scientific explanation will not bring him peace, but the right gesture might help.

If we kiss the picture of someone we love, we are not trying to have an effect on the loved one. The kiss does not *aim* at anything; we act in this way and then feel satisfied.

So, it is the *spirit in which one acts* that is vital, and the notion of language games clarifies this.

One would not conduct a love affair in the same manner as one would a funeral.

You don't investigate whether your partner loves you or not in the same spirit as a scientific investigation.

OSCAR ZARATE

The notion of language games makes one attend to the spirit in which we act, and so throws light on magic.

FAMILY RESEMBLANCES

"The more narrowly we examine actual language, the sharper becomes the conflict between it and our requirement... We have got onto slippery ice where there is no friction and so in a certain sense the conditions are ideal, but also, just because of that, we are unable to walk. We want to walk: so we need *friction*. Back to the rough ground!" (**PI** 107)

When we start thinking about the meaning of "life", "time", "space", "mind", "body", "meaning", "free-will", "the good", and other grand philosophical questions, we become bewitched by language.

We take the words out of their natural place in talking and assume they refer to some essence or ideal entity which we try to define.

Because the word is uniform in appearance, we assume it refers to a uniform entity about which we can generalize.

We forget the **application** of the word.

Take the word "good". What is common between a good joke, a good tennis player, a good man, feeling good, good will, good breeding, good looking, and a good for nothing?

There is no one common property which the word **good** refers to.

We cannot analyze the word so that we reach some essence or element from which the concept is built up.

> But there are resemblances between the various meanings of the term— like family resemblances.

When we look at the members of a family, we can see that they can have certain features in common, like facial features, colour and type of hair, gait, temperament, manner of speaking and so on.

We give examples of similarities and do not attempt to define them, as there are no sharp boundaries.

It is like a rope; its strength does not lie in any one fibre but in the overlapping of many.

ROOTS OR BULBS?

Language games and family resemblances are central notions in Wittgenstein's later thought and make his thought *rhizomatic* rather than *arboreal*.

Most traditional philosophy is like a tree. It seeks the roots from which its object is constructed. It wants to find the founding principle of things, and so account for the different and irregular in terms of the same or regular, to bring the unruly under one rule.

A rhizome (bulbs and tubers), on the other hand, is more like a network, a multiplicity, which has diverse forms ramifying in all directions.

Any point on it can be connected with any other.

EVOLUTIONARY TREE

There is no ideal point closed on itself that serves as a foundation. It changes its nature as it increases in connections, but follows lines.

It can be cracked and broken, but it starts off again following another of its lines.

It is not answerable to any structural or generative model.

The notion of family resemblance is particularly important in considering psychological concepts.

We have already seen some of the complexities of "thought". But "know", "wish", "intend", "believe", "mean" are not defined by characteristic marks either.

What is going on in your mind when you are wishing or intending, for example?

You can't point to a specific experience of wishing or intending, for they do not differ in the content of experience, but are radically different types of concept.

The **circumstances** in which the words are used give the clue.

Specificity does not belong to the **experience** but to the **language game** which enables us to talk about or express our desires, intentions, meanings, etc.

These are a **family of cases**, for they are all "in the mind", but they have complex kinships with each other.

Meaning depends on articulation rather than representation.

What is specific is always a function of the language game and can only be articulated within it.

MATHEMATICS AND RULES

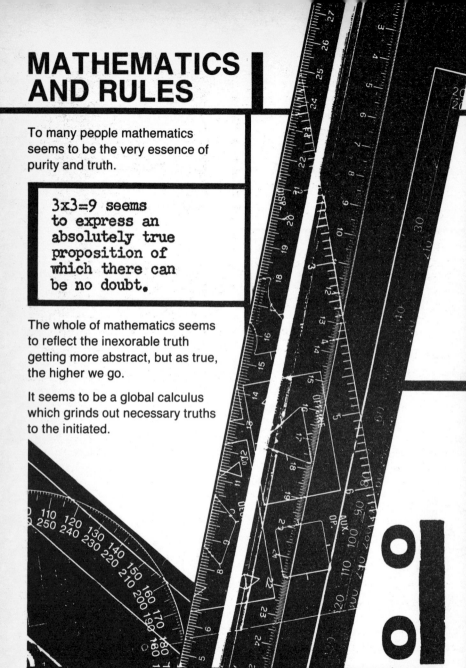

To many people mathematics seems to be the very essence of purity and truth.

3x3=9 seems to express an absolutely true proposition of which there can be no doubt.

The whole of mathematics seems to reflect the inexorable truth getting more abstract, but as true, the higher we go.

It seems to be a global calculus which grinds out necessary truths to the initiated.

Furthermore, it seems that there must be a domain of objects that these propositions are **true of**. We can't see them — you can't see the set of all natural numbers for example — so these objects must be **ideal.**

We come to think that mathematics is the natural history of these "ideal objects". And many philosophers have occupied themselves in seeking or creating the foundations of this crystal palace.

In his many remarks on mathematics, Wittgenstein is concerned to show the delusiveness of this picture. For when we reflect on it, we forget that we are looking at a projection of our own decisions and their consequences.

The mathematician is an inventor, not a discoverer.

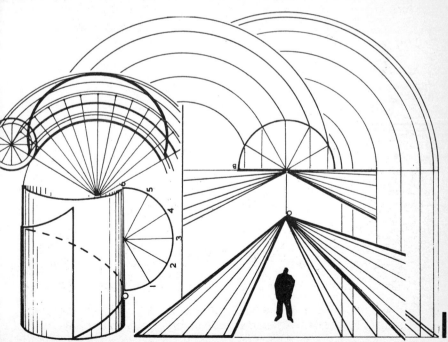

> Mathematics has not got a foundation in "set theory" or in any other theory. It depends on our *form of life*.

If we were intelligent extra-terrestrials who "saw" only in the infra-red end of the spectrum, who got around only by squirming, who found it easier to visualize a Klein bottle in four-dimensional space than a torus in three dimesions, and for whom dissonance was a delight, then we would have a different mathematics.

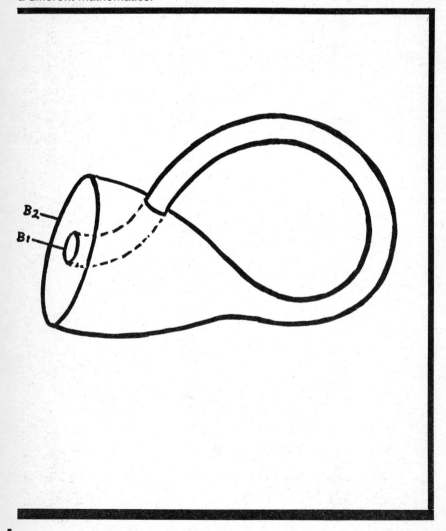

In our form of life, rulers are not elastic; children are trained in elementary arithmetic, they learn it by rote; certain patterns like circles, squares and symmetries are memorable; periodic phenomena and rhythm attract us, music and mathematics are closely related; and so on.

Mathematics depends on
these facts of our lives.

Mathematics, like games and language, depends on our ability to follow **rules**.

When we calculate, we use rules, when we speak we follow rules of grammar and pronunciation, and games involve rules.

Reason itself is constituted by rules, for rules constitute an individual's *reason for doing things*.

Most importantly, rules and their applications are varied. They are a family of cases. And they must have a public context in which obedience to them makes sense.

We must learn to attend to the shifts in the meaning and context of following a rule.

Here are some examples.

You are in a
playing field
with your eyes
bandaged, and
someone leads
you by the hand,
sometimes left,
sometimes right;
you have constantly
to be ready for
the tug of his hand,
and must also take
care not to stumble
when he gives an
unexpected tug.

Someone leads you
by the hand where
you are unwilling
to go, by force.

You are guided by
a partner in a dance.
You make yourself as
receptive as possible
in order to guess his
intention and obey
the slightest pressure.

Someone takes you for
a walk; you are having
a conversation; you go
wherever he does.

You walk along
a field track, simply
following it.

Wittgenstein tries to show that mathematics depends on using mathematical symbols correctly and the nuances of rule-following. Far from being a crystal palace reaching to the sky and resting on concrete foundations, mathematics is more like a rhizome, a motley of different cases of rule-following, of subtle shifts, as we move from fibre to fibre in its thread.

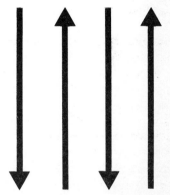

THE INNER AND THE OUTER

What goes on "inside" a person when he or she thinks and feels?

What is behind that smile — or is it a smirk?

In trying to answer these questions, we tend to picture an "inner world". But where is it? In the head? In the brain? And what are its contents? Thoughts, feelings and desires?

But one finds no thoughts or feelings in the brain.

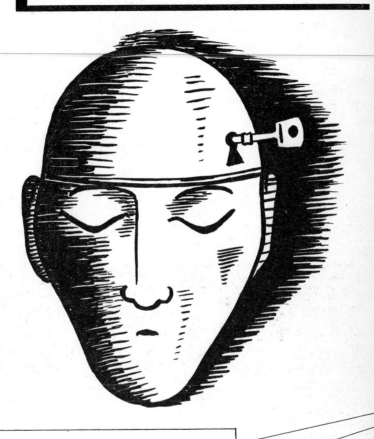

It seems that the inner world of consciousness is a succession of private experiences, known by its possessor alone.

It follows that we can only infer other people's inner world.

This picture of the mind, which is raised to a dogma in much psychology and psychoanalysis, is the target for many of Wittgenstein's remarks.

For example, if I am to observe my desires, I must already know what they are, in order to observe them. And how can I be sure that observing them does not alter them?

And how do we know that other people mean the same when they talk of the contents of their consciousness as we do?

It is obvious that we can keep our thoughts, feelings and desires to ourselves.

I may hate my boss and wish him dead, but may consider it wiser to keep it to myself. He might guess as much from subtle gestures that I inadvertently make, but my thoughts would not be revealed to him.

OSCAR ZARATE

But keeping thoughts and feelings to myself does not mean that I put or keep them anywhere. I simply do not express them.

We cannot find what is in other people's minds, as we can find what is in their pockets.

A guessing game of what is in your mind would not be much of a party game — but lovers can play it. Why so?

Lovers EXPRESS their feelings and thoughts to one another. But when they do this, their words are not an outward sign of an inner state.

They do not have to first know what they think or feel, and then state it.

Their thoughts and feelings are sincere, and are therefore manifest to one another in the language game of their words and gestures.

Whereas at a party one would know what one had thought,
keep it secret, and then admit it or tell a lie if someone guessed it.

But no one else
could know for
certain what I
actually thought,
because a different
language game from
expressing thoughts
sincerely is being
played.

When we express our thoughts and desires, they do not lie in some inner world waiting to be expressed, so that we can be right or wrong about what to express.

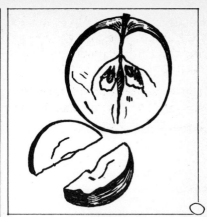

For example, when we express the wish for an apple, we can't make a mistake and find that really the wish, lying in the inner world, was for a banana!

But of course we can and often do deceive ourselves and others about our feelings and desires.

But deceiving or pretending is not the same as making a mistake about what is in the inner world.

142

We can say that we don't know what we want, think or feel. This does not mean that I want 'x' and don't know it, but rather that I haven't *decided* what I want or feel.

The language games of deceiving and deciding are very different from that of making mistakes about what is present or not "in the mind".

This can be made clearer by considering pain.

The experience of feeling pain is not that there is an "I" that has something.

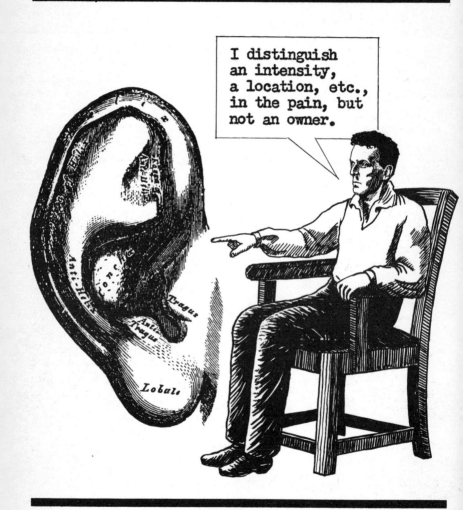

What sort of a thing would pain be that no one HAS? Pain belonging to no one at all?

you not hear the Aziola cry?
Methinks ... nigh,
Said
dusk, ere s
An
This Azio
Asked
I felt to
No

And lau

Sad

By

S

Sad Aziola!
Loved thee and thy sad cry.

brought;
woman,
ow elate
thing human,
fear or hate:
soul,
quiet yourself
little downy o

ntide
ard
eadow and m
rshes wide,—
lute, nor win
rred;
ter than them
hat moment I

If I say, "I am in pain", I do not choose the mouth which says "I".

I cannot be in error as to who is suffering from the pain.

It makes no sense to ask: "How do you know it is you who are in pain?"

The phrase, "I am in pain", is a pain signal and not a reference to pain processes going on inside me.

The expression "I am sad", on the other hand, is not a signal but the expression of a particular pattern in human life.

My sadness could, for example, be expressed in a poem.

FIRST AND THIRD PERSONS

There is an asymmetry between the concepts of the **1st person** and **3rd person** which has important consequences.

It seems that we know our own experiences, whereas we have to infer other people's.

To say "I know that I am in pain" is a logical and meaningful proposition, but it is senseless because I neither know it nor do I not know it!

Knowledge is connected with doubt and certainty, learning and finding out, grounds and confirmation. These cannot apply to my own pain.

But it makes good sense to say "I know he is in pain", for here I can find out and be wrong.

We have a deep tendency to model our awareness of our own pains, desires and feelings on our awareness of others. The phrases: "**I** am in pain" and "**He** is in pain" have similar form but different uses.

Our relation to ourselves is not one of observation. If we are in pain, we are <u>in</u> it, whereas <u>we</u> may have to infer other people's.

We may at times not be sure what to call our sensations.

If you slowly stick
a pin into your skin,
there may be a certain
point at which you are
uncertain whether you
are in discomfort
or pain.

But you are sure you are having the **sensation**, and no further evidence
will tell you if it is pain or discomfort.

A little later you might say, "I know this IS pain", and this makes sense
because the knowledge is of the **expression** not the sensation.

We may say: "I know what I think" or "I know what I feel", meaning I know what my position is.

Thus at a party someone gushes...

Here I am referring to what I have thought, not claiming knowledge of what I am thinking.

The endless confusions about the inner and outer can be clarified by careful attention to the language games being played when we speak to one another.

Understanding involves not only direct knowledge but imponderable evidence.

The possibility of pretence, our own particular sensitivities and blindnesses, nuances of gesture, time – all play a part.

Think of the Mona Lisa's smile, or telling a smile from a grin or a sneer or a smirk.

Can you prove that a certain gesture is genuine?

How do you know someone is pleased to see you?

How do you know that someone loves you or that you love them?

It is not by observing the intensity of the feeling.

Here we need subtle outer criteria, for love is put to the test over time. It is not just a "feeling" we can identify.

Can you love a person for one hour, and after that be totally indifferent to them?

The inner is not hidden, but the language game we play in expressing ourselves is one where certainty is excluded.

The inner is not a brute reality which can be mapped out by psychologists, but a tangle of concepts relating the inner to the outer which lies at the heart of human understanding.

If we knew for certain what others felt, if their minds were totally transparent to us, then human life as we know it would cease.

Psychological therapies in this century have claimed to know either the outer (behavourism) or the inner (psychoanalysis).

In contrast, Wittgenstein's therapy is concerned not so much with knowledge as with clarifying the language games weaving the inner to the outer.

SEEING ASPECTS

In the last few years of his life Wittgenstein wrote on **aspect seeing**. If we look at a schematic drawing such as the duck-rabbit we first see it, say, as a duck and then the aspect changes and we see it as a rabbit. Or we may see a tree in a puzzle picture, and then discover a thief in the branches. Or we may see a face, and then see its likeness to another.

In music we may hear a tune, and then hear its likeness to a bird singing, as in "programme" music.

In all these cases, there is a paradox, for in seeing the aspect change we see the figure *differently*, yet the total perception has not changed.

Aspect-seeing brings out the complications of perceiving, knowing and interpreting.

When we see tables and chairs and other familiar objects, we do not see them **as** a table or **as** a chair. We see tables and chairs.

But if someone from a culture that had no word for table, as it had no use for them, called my table an "altar" in his language, then we could say that I see it as a table and he sees it as an altar.

But what is "it"?

Is there a pure sense impression or *inner picture* that can be separated from an interpretation?

Do these ancient paradigms of sensation-versus-thought or interpretation really work?

Both things — the report and the exclamation — are expressions of perception and of visual experience. But the exclamation is so in a different sense from the report. It is forced from us. It is related to the experience as a cry is to pain.

154

When we cry, "It's a rabbit", we are expressing an experience. This is to be contrasted with ordinary perception where we give descriptions or reports of what we see or hear.

We take for granted that the objects we encounter are of a certain kind, and we know our way amongst them.

In aspect perception we express an experience.

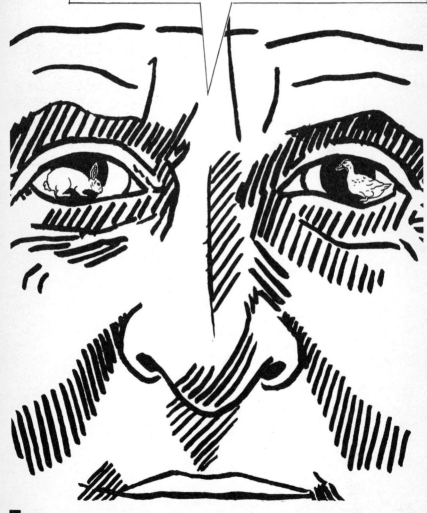

> There are many ways of experiencing aspects. What they have in common is the expression: "Now I see it as THAT"; or "Now I see it THIS way"; or "Now it's THIS — now THAT"; or "Now I hear it as ....; a while ago I heard it as ....".

But the explanation for these "*thats*" and "*this ways*" is radically different in the different cases.

When we see an aspect and exclaim, we are not describing an experience but making a spontaneous verbal gesture which is the primary expression of the experience.

So there is not *first* the seeing of something, and *then* an interpretation of it.

There is a difference between a **report** about what has been seen and the **expression** of a visual experience, but that does not mean that aspect seeing is an interpretation that takes place "on top of" normal seeing.

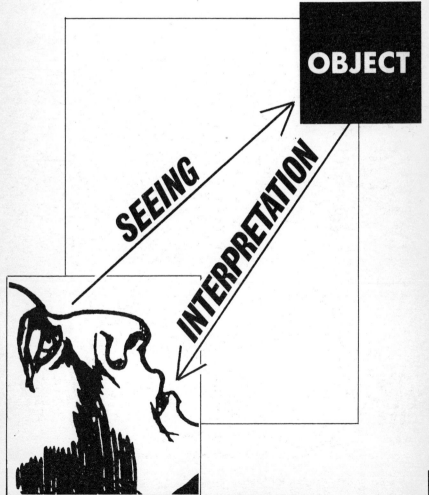

MEANING BLINDNESS

Part of the importance of aspect perception lies in the fact that **words** can be the focus of aspect perception. For words can **mean** in different ways. Puns and word play are examples.

Thus:

> They went and
> told the sexton
> And the sexton
> tolled the bell.

or:

> He bolted
> the door
> and his
> dinner.

or: when Mercutio is bleeding to death, Shakespeare has him say...
"Ask for me tomorrow and you shall find me a grave man."

Wittgenstein was fond of punning in his letters.

A meaning-blind person
is one who cannot experience
the double meaning of these puns.

He can only understand one meaning at a time, and so they aren't amusing.

He is like a person with no sense of humour. He can understand the explanation of a joke but cannot laugh.

He can hear music but does not have a musical ear.

He can deduce what a picture represents but cannot see it directly as the object it depicts.

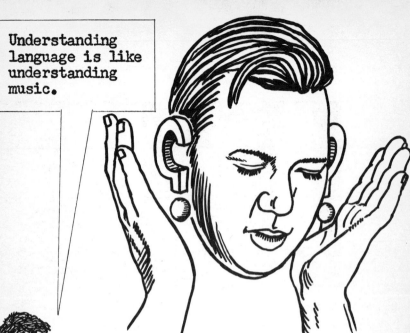

Understanding language is like understanding music.

Language can convey information, and music cannot, but both are expressive and require subtle responses to convey understanding. These responses do not depend on explicit rules, but on appropriate responses to the aspects, their differences and similarities.

The sound of words, their associations, their "look" and history are all important in expressing meaning.

Take the words "friend", "comrade", "mate", "pal", "buddy". They all have a similar meaning but have a very different "look". It would sound strange if the Queen in a speech referred to her "friend" as a "buddy".

The fact that we can experience the meaning of words enables us to use language creatively.

When a word is used outside its usual context, then new meanings are created.

Thus a child may first respond to pain by saying "Ow", but later it learns to call pains "throbbing", "piercing", "like needles" and so on.

Taking words that are appropriate on a certain occasion and giving them a new use is important in characterizing our feelings.

Poetry depends greatly on this ability. A meaning-blind person cannot appreciate it.

A meaning-blind person lacks neither a kind of sense experience nor mastery in speaking and giving explanations, but a **sensibility**. He cannot experience meaning.

If I compare the coming of the MEANING into one's mind to a dream, then our talk is ordinarily dreamless. The "meaning-blind" man would then be one who would always talk dreamlessly.

The meaning-blind person has lost touch with language as an expressive medium.

He can say what he intends to say but cannot experience the meaning of the gestures which are an essential part of the expression of our experience.

He is condemned to an impoverished inner life.

If a person is hurt by unkind words, intrigued by subtle points, has a sense of humour, is touched by sad stories, fears death, then we might say he has "a soul".

Shared human reactions and gestures underlie the language game connected with "soul talk".

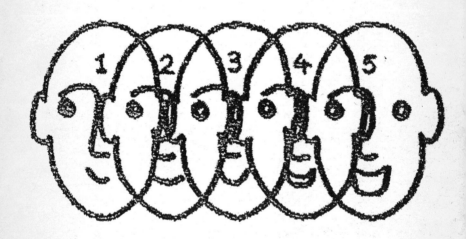

If when someone "smiled", he had only five positions of his face, and when it changed it snapped straight from one position to another, then we might not be able to respond to him as we do to a smile, and we might then wonder if he had a soul.

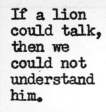

If a lion
could talk,
then we
could not
understand
him.

Hi folks!

Thus if he shouted
"Hi, folks!" at feeding
time at the zoo, we would
not know how to take his
remark, although it is
correct English, as we
do not share his form
of life.

Only a human-looking lion as in a
cartoon would make sense.

165

CERTAINTY

In the last two years of his life, when he knew he was dying, Wittgenstein wrote on the theme of certainty.

In the Western tradition, philosophers have assumed that our knowledge is based on fundamental items which must be taken as self-evident. If this cannot be done, then the whole edifice of knowledge might be uncertain and total scepticism would reign. We would not even know whether we were dreaming or not!

René Descartes' proposition, *cogito ergo sum* — I think therefore I am — is a famous example of supposedly reaching bedrock.

G. E. Moore, Wittgenstein's predecessor in the Cambridge chair of philosophy, had tried to allay sceptical doubt about all knowledge by holding up his hands at a lecture and saying, with suitable gestures...

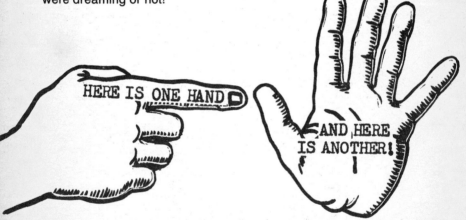

HERE IS ONE HAND

AND HERE IS ANOTHER!

...concluding from this, that he knew for certain there **are** things external to the mind. He was not just dreaming.

Wittgenstein, in his remarks collected in **On Certainty**, questioned Moore's conclusion.

Moore produced propositions that he claimed to know for certain. There are many such propositions, for example, "I am a human being", "I am sitting writing at a desk", "I have not been to Mars", "I am alive", "The earth existed long before I was born", and so on.

Under normal circumstances these propositions would not be remarked upon or doubted.

In exceptional circumstances, they would be. Thus, there may come a time when most people HAVE visited Mars. Very depressed people sometimes say they are dead. People sometimes feel they are inhuman, etc. Even a philosopher's questions have their place.

I am sitting with a philosopher in the garden; he says again and again "I know that that's a tree", pointing to a tree that is near us. Someone else arrives and hears this, and I tell him: "This fellow isn't insane. We are only doing philosophy." (**OC** 467).

Now, ordinarily, when we say we know something, we can give compelling reasons for it. But when a philosopher says he knows he is holding his hand in front of him, he can give no reason that is as certain as the very thing it is meant to be a reason for.

My having two hands is not less certain before I have looked at them than afterwards.

What reply does one make to someone who says, "I believe it merely strikes you as if you know it?"

So to say "I know" in these circumstances is senseless.

Our aim must be to avoid countering the assertion that one cannot know that (that's a hand or a tree), by saying, "I do know it."

We must steer a path between the sceptic's doubt as to whether we know anything at all, and Moore's dogmatism in claiming that he does know basic things for certain.

RIVER-BED PROPOSITIONS

The basic propositions we have been discussing are called **river-bed propositions.** They are taken for granted in ordinary conversation and create the framework of our ordinary behaviour. They express the stable but not fixed background on which the practices of questioning and learning depend.

A child, for example, has to participate in an activity, a language game, before it can use words like "know", "believe" and "be certain".

A child fetches books and sits in chairs long before it can understand whether or not these things exist and whether it can be certain.

But can a child be said to *know* that a tree exists?

Does a child *believe* that milk exists? Or does it *know* that milk exists?

Does a cat know that a mouse exists?

Wittgenstein was fond of J. W. von Goethe's saying, "In the beginning was the deed." It is not knowledge but primitive actions and reactions that are vital for concept-formation and the later development of knowledge.

River-bed propositions are not part of the "traffic" of ordinary talk, but are presupposed by it. Nor do they form the foundations of knowledge as have been sought by traditional philosophers. They are hidden parts of a changing multiplicity, a rhizome, rather than a fixed set of fundamental beliefs on which knowledge can be built.

Wittgenstein was particularly fond of Leo Tolstoy's short story, "The Three Hermits", from **Twenty-three Tales** (1886). It illustrated for him the depth and seriousness of philosophical problems.

A bishop on a voyage saw a fisherman pointing.

The bishop could make out nothing but water shimmering in the sun. Eventually, he saw the island and asked to visit it for a few hours.

He found three old men holding hands. One was small and always smiling. The second was taller and strong, kindly and cheerful. The third was tall and stern.

The bishop smiled and spent the rest of the day trying to teach them the prayer, "Our Father".

The bishop returned to his ship and sailed away. When it was dark, he sat at the stern gazing at the sea where the island had disappeared.

Suddenly, he saw something white and shining on the bright path which the moon cast on the water.

This light rapidly got nearer, until he could see it was the three hermits gliding on the water.

FURTHER READING

Books by Wittgenstein
The only philosophy book written by him is difficult for the ordinary reader because of its use of logical symbols: **Tractatus Logico-Philosophicus**, Routledge and Kegan Paul, London 1961.
A friendlier collection of his remarks is **Philosophical Investigations**, B. Blackwell, Oxford 1958.
A very readable collection of his thoughts on culture, the arts, history and religion is **Culture and Value**, B. Blackwell, Oxford 1980, and also a collection of his notes made in the last year of his life, **On Certainty**, B. Blackwell, Oxford 1969.
There are also many other collections of his notes on mathematics, psychology, colour, anthropology and logic, as well as notes made on his lectures by students and collections of some of his letters.

Books on Wittgenstein
Much has been written on Wittgenstein's thought. A. Kenny, **Wittgenstein**, Penguin 1973, is a good orthodox account. J. Schulte, **Wittgenstein: An Introduction**, State University of New York Press, 1992, is perhaps the best introduction to date. For those who want to tackle the **Tractatus**, try H.O. Mounce, **Wittgenstein's Tractatus: An Introduction**, B. Blackwell, Oxford 1981.
G.P. Baker and P.M.S. Hacker, **Wittgenstein: An Analytic Commentary on the Philosophical Investigations**, B. Blackwell, Oxford, is a 4-volume, 2000-page study! Readable, clear, but for enthusiasts only.
S. Cavell, **The Claim of Reason**, Clarendon Press, Oxford 1979, is a thoughtful book on the relation of Wittgenstein to scepticism, morality and tragedy.
H. Staten, **Wittgenstein and Derrida**, B. Blackwell, Oxford 1985, discusses Wittgenstein's relation to deconstruction.
G. Frongia and B. McGuinness, **Wittgenstein: A Bibliographical Guide**, B. Blackwell, Oxford 1990. An invaluable guide to all the articles on Wittgenstein to 1990.

Biography
Wittgenstein's personality had a special fascination, and many memoirs have been written, as well as poems, paintings and music inspired by him. The best known is Norman Malcolm's **Wittgenstein: A Memoir**, Oxford University Press, 1984. Thomas Bernhard's novel, **Wittgenstein's Nephew**, Quartet Books, 1986, is by a master of contemporary fiction and worth reading.

The best biography is Ray Monk's **Ludwig Wittgenstein: The Duty of Genius**, J. Cape, London 1990, and is very readable.
For a good account of the **Tractatus** and its links with Wittgenstein's life, consult Brian McGuinness, **Wittgenstein: A Life. Young Ludwig (1889-1921)**, Penguin 1988.
To grasp the breadth of Wittgenstein's thought, one should read F. Dostoyevsky's **The Brothers Karamazov** and G. Frege's **The Foundations of Arithmetic**, both of which he knew practically off by heart.

Acknowledgements

This book is a rhizome, an arrangement of heterogeneous seeds that have grown from Wittgenstein's soil. So many people have inadvertently contributed to it. I would like to have mentioned the various translators of Wittgenstein and his commentators, but they are too numerous to list. I should however mention P.M.S. Hacker, B. McGuinness, S. Cavell and P. Winch whose work has been especially helpful to me. I thank the publisher Junghens-Verlag, Cuxhaven, for permission to reproduce the diagram on page 31, from their book by E.M. Lange, **Wittgenstein und Schopenhauer**, 1989, and Michael Hamburger the translator of Georg Trakl's poem, **Grodek**, part of which I have quoted.
John Heaton

Judy Groves thanks Oscar Zarate, Josephine King, Reuben Knutson and Howard Peters for help with picture research and artwork.

John Heaton studied natural sciences and moral sciences at Trinity College, Cambridge, attending lectures by Bertrand Russell. He subsequently trained in psychotherapy and worked for some 20 years with R.D. Laing in the Philadelphia Association. He is a founder member of the Guild of Psychotherapy. He has published many articles and papers including a number on philosophy and its relationship to therapy.

Judy Groves is a painter, illustrator and designer working mainly in the area of human rights and environmental issues. Her paintings and prints have been exhibited in London and Rome. She is also the illustrator of **Jesus for Beginners**.